Be Water, My Friend

The Early Years of Bruce Lee

by **Ken Mochizuki** • illustrated by **Dom Lee**

Lee & Low Books Inc.
New York

Like flowing water, Bruce Lee could never be still.

Neither could his father, who was always on the move. An acclaimed performer with Hong Kong's Cantonese Opera Company, he was on a tour of the United States with his wife when Bruce was born in San Francisco in 1940.

His father made Bruce an actor when he was still a baby. Bruce first appeared in a movie when he was just three months old. After the family returned to Hong Kong in 1941, Bruce began acting in more movies. Soon he was performing backflips and cartwheels. Bruce didn't think they were hard to do at all.

Bruce grew up in a second-story apartment with his sisters and brothers, an aunt, cousins, and a few birds, dogs, and fish. He loved playing practical jokes, like rearranging tables and chairs so others would stumble over them at night. He was always talking, always running around. Bruce's family nicknamed him *Mo Si Tung*, which means "never sits still" in English.

There was one thing that kept Bruce still for hours—books. He loved myths and legends—stories of warrior heroes who fought for the oppressed and who possessed abilities no others had. He read during the day and even in the dark. Bruce's eyesight got so bad, he had to wear thick eyeglasses by age six.

Even though Bruce loved reading, school bored him. He couldn't stay still. He would rather go to opera rehearsals or film sets with his father or practice dancing with his mother. When everyone was away, his mother would clear some space in the apartment and teach Bruce ballroom dancing. He loved the smooth and uninterrupted flow as they moved across the floor.

Sometimes Bruce's family was invited to fancy parties. If his father was traveling, Bruce's mother had no one to dance with her. Bruce hated seeing that.

"Madam," he would say, "would you like to dance?"

Bruce often skipped school, preferring to roam the streets of Hong Kong alone. With his father rarely home, Bruce's mother had to deal with his misbehavior. She scolded Bruce, asking how he expected to make a living in the future if he didn't get an education.

Bruce replied that he didn't need to go to school. "I'll become a famous film star one day," he said.

His mother scoffed. The life of a film star was not as easy and glamorous as he imagined, she told Bruce. He first needed to finish school like everyone else.

As Bruce grew older, school got tougher. At that time, Hong Kong was a colony of Great Britain, so classes at his school were taught in English. The books were in English too. Bruce didn't always understand what the teachers said, and the books might as well have been written in code.

Bruce looked forward to joining his friends at the end of the day. They teased, heckled, and challenged some of their schoolmates, as well as students from other schools. They got into fights. Bruce and his friends found out that picking on kids bigger than themselves was a mistake!

In Hong Kong the martial arts were as popular as baseball was in the United States. Some of Bruce's friends knew a few of the moves. Some just copied others. Bruce decided he really wanted to learn martial arts from a master.

The best martial arts master in Hong Kong was Yip Man. The master knew Bruce's father was a popular performer, and he knew of Bruce too as a young movie actor. But being from a well-known family did not guarantee study with a master. Yip Man wanted to know if Bruce was serious about learning martial arts.

"Allow me to learn like anyone else," Bruce told Yip Man, "and I will become your most dedicated student."

At the master's school Bruce didn't have to sit. He had to use his entire body, and he loved it. New students spent hours practicing the right stance, and Yip Man wouldn't teach a new technique until students mastered the one they were learning. One of the most important exercises students were drilled in was "sticking hands," the art of wrapping up an opponent's hands and arms.

Sometimes Bruce trained for four to six hours a day. After months of intense concentration, sweat, and bruises, he didn't have to think about what he was doing. The moves became automatic.

Bruce soon became one of Yip Man's top students. Outside the master's school Bruce kicked leaves off trees to build up his leg muscles. He pounded on a stool during dinner to strengthen his hands.

Then one day after school Bruce joined his friends and used what he had learned to fight others.

When Bruce arrived for his lessons the next day, Yip Man ignored him. The master helped other students but not Bruce. Finally, Bruce asked what he was doing wrong.

"You have misused what you are being taught," the master told Bruce sternly. "You are really being taught the discipline of *not* having to fight."

"Then what are martial arts for?" Bruce asked.

Yip Man continued to ignore him. This made Bruce mad, and he took it out on other students. The master saw everything. He asked Bruce to meet with him alone.

"There are such things as harmony and yielding in martial arts," Yip Man explained. "Big branches of a tree snap under the weight of snow, while weaker and suppler reeds bend and survive." He told Bruce to relax, calm his mind, forget about himself. "Do not interfere with the natural flow," the master continued. "There is even gentleness in martial arts."

"Gentleness?" Bruce responded. "How can I relax and be calm while exchanging blows and kicks?"

Yip Man told Bruce to think about what he had said and not to come to his lessons for a week.

Bruce practiced by himself even more and thought deeply about what the master had told him. No answers came, so he gave up and went out in a boat alone.

Gentleness? Bruce asked himself for the hundredth time. It didn't make sense. Because he did not understand, did it mean that all the training was for nothing?

Angry with himself, Bruce punched the water. *Wait a minute. . . .*

Bruce struck the water again. No matter how hard he hit the water, he couldn't shatter it. He tried to grab the water, but it ran right out of his hands.

Water, the softest substance on Earth, could never be hurt because it offered no resistance. But with enough force it could break through anything in the world.

Bruce let the boat drift, for it was useless to fight the water.

"Gentleness . . . I think I understand," Bruce told Yip Man when he returned to his lessons. "But how is it applied?"

"Let us begin," the master said.

After almost four years, Bruce began to understand gentleness and yielding, and how to expend the least amount of energy while using the opponent's energy against him—that less is more. Those concepts may have sounded easy, but Bruce found out that to apply them was not.

A teacher at Bruce's high school, a former boxer who recognized Bruce's athletic abilities, encouraged him to compete in Hong Kong's interschool boxing championship.

Why not? Bruce thought confidently. *How different can it be from martial arts?*

Bruce made it to the final match, using the boxing skills he had taught himself from watching other students, but his last opponent was the three-time defending champion. Bruce soon discovered why. The champ pushed Bruce around the ring. Trying to be as tough, Bruce let loose with a flurry of punches. They all fell short. Bruce could only shield himself as he was forced backward. Then he found himself on the ropes.

Bruce began to see the match as if he were a spectator, watching himself lose to a bigger and stronger opponent.

Suddenly Bruce's arms flew out, wrapping up his opponent's hands and arms. As the champ frantically tried to untangle himself, Bruce wrapped him up again.

What just happened? Bruce asked himself. *Sticking hands!*

He doesn't know what that is! Bruce realized. He calmed himself, saving his energy as his opponent danced around. Bruce followed the natural flow, expanding as his opponent contracted, contracting as his opponent expanded. If he offered no resistance, the champ had nothing to hit.

Bruce moved in close and parried a jab. The rest was automatic.

Contact!

Quick! Sticking hands again!

That's it!

Bruce scored a knockout and won the championship.

Now that Bruce was the champion, he had many new friends. They asked Bruce to teach them what he had done in the boxing ring. At the same time there were students who wanted to fight him. Bruce wouldn't back down from a challenge, and his temper got him into trouble.

Bruce's mother had to go to the police station and sign a statement that
said she was responsible for his future conduct. When his father returned home,
his parents decided that Bruce should leave Hong Kong for a fresh start somewhere
else. Bruce finally realized how badly he had let them down. His mother pressed
a hundred-dollar bill into his hand and folded his fingers around it.

Bruce Lee's youth ended then, at age eighteen. He was alone, on a ship sailing back to the United States. His parents had arranged for him to stay in San Francisco with friends of theirs.

Bruce knew he still had a lot to learn. He shouldn't have been in those fights in the first place, misusing what Yip Man had taught him. He promised himself that in America he would conduct himself differently. All his martial arts training would count for something.

Bruce watched the swirling water from the deck of the ship. He saw how water always found a way around an obstacle and continued on. Bruce calmed his mind and forgot about himself. He joined the gentle, natural flow.

"Be water, my friend."

The Rest of Bruce Lee's Story

1959–1964

In every passionate pursuit, the pursuit counts more than the object pursued.—Bruce Lee

Bruce Lee regretted not taking school seriously. In the United States he had to catch up in order to receive his high school diploma. He then attended the University of Washington in Seattle, where he loved studying philosophy. Bruce also gave classes in the martial art called kung fu. He taught that kung fu could instill self-confidence, humility, adaptability, and respect for others in those who studied it.

His goal was to establish martial arts schools all over America.

One of Bruce's students was Linda Emery. She and Bruce began dating during a time when interracial dating and marriage were not common or popular. After fighting for approval from Linda's family, Bruce and Linda married in 1964. They later had a son, Brandon, and a daughter, Shannon.

1965–1970

The greatest help is self-help.—Bruce Lee

Bruce and his family moved to Oakland and then to Los Angeles, California. After amazing an audience at a martial arts tournament, Bruce won the role of Kato on the mid-1960s television series *The Green Hornet*. The series lasted less than a year, but it showcased Bruce's martial arts ability and lightning-quick reflexes.

After *The Green Hornet*, Bruce found few acting jobs, especially since he refused to play parts that stereotyped Asians. He returned to teaching martial arts and strove to improve his own skills, always practicing, always learning, always reading from his library of twenty-five hundred books. He borrowed from other martial arts, sports, and Eastern and Western philosophies and created his own martial art called *jeet kune do*.

Bruce still wanted to act, but the message from Hollywood was always the same. He was too short, he did not have enough acting experience, and a Chinese person could never be a star in America.

1971–1973

To change with change is the changeless state.—Bruce Lee

Bruce returned to Hong Kong and discovered that he was a movie star there. *The Green Hornet*, renamed *The Kato Show*, was shown on television repeatedly, as were the movies he had appeared in as a youth. Bruce began acting in movies again, now as the martial artist he had become. He was the hero, playing characters who fought for the oppressed and who possessed abilities no others had.

Bruce also taught himself to make his own films, and eventually he starred in a major American/Hong Kong co-production, *Enter the Dragon*. Only by becoming a star in Asia did he get to play the lead in an American film.

Before the release of *Enter the Dragon* in 1973, Bruce Lee died suddenly due to fluid collecting around his brain. He was thirty-two years old. The movie went on to become a huge hit in the United States and Asia. Bruce Lee was finally a star in America.

For the enduring legacy of Bruce Lee—human being—K.M.

To the Bruce Lee fans from all over the world. You are the ones
who keep his legend alive—D.L.

SOURCES

Bruce Lee: A Warrior's Journey. DVD. Directed by John Little. Burbank, CA: Warner Home Video, 2001.

The Bruce Lee Collectors Exhibit Commemorative Program, 2003. Published in conjunction with the exhibition
"The Bruce Lee Collectors Exhibit 2003: The Beginning of a Legend, The Story of a Man." Seattle, WA.

Chunovic, Louis. *Bruce Lee: The Tao of the Dragon Warrior*. New York: St. Martin Griffin, 1996.

Clouse, Robert. *Bruce Lee: The Biography*. Burbank, CA: Unique Publications, 1988.

Koopmans, Andy. *The Importance of Bruce Lee*. San Diego, CA: Lucent Books, 2002.

Lee, Bruce. "Bruce Lee: In His Own Words." Special Features/Documentaries. *Enter the Dragon*: Special Edition.
2 DVD. Directed by Robert Clouse. Burbank, CA: Warner Home Video, 1998.

——. *Bruce Lee: The Celebrated Life of the Golden Dragon*. Edited by John Little. Boston: Tuttle Publishing, 2000.

——. *The Tao of Jeet Kune Do*. Santa Clarita, CA: Ohara Publications, 1975.

Lee, Linda, and Tom Bleecker. *The Bruce Lee Story*. Santa Clarita, CA: Ohara Publications, 1989.

Tagliaferro, Linda. *Bruce Lee*. Minneapolis: Lerner Publications, 2000.

AUTHOR'S NOTE

This story is true to the facts of Bruce Lee's life. Due to limited information about Lee's earliest years, some events are extensions of the facts based on the author's knowledge of the times and circumstances of Lee's life.

The title *Be Water, My Friend* is a direct quote from Bruce Lee.

The calligraphy on the back jacket is the character for "dragon." Bruce Lee was often called "Dragon" because he was born during the hour and year of the dragon. Later the nickname was used in the titles of many of Lee's martial arts films, including his most famous, *Enter the Dragon*.

Text copyright © 2006 by Ken Mochizuki
Illustrations copyright © 2006 by Dom Lee

All rights reserved. No part of the contents of this book may be reproduced
by any means without the written permission of the publisher.
LEE & LOW BOOKS Inc., 95 Madison Avenue, New York, NY 10016
leeandlow.com

Manufactured in China

Book design by Susan & David Neuhaus/NeuStudio
Book production by The Kids at Our House

The text is set in Rotis SemiSerif
The illustrations are rendered by applying acrylic on paper, melting encaustic
beeswax over it, and scratching the images out of the wax.

10 9 8 7 6 5 4 3 2 1
First Edition

Library of Congress Cataloging-in-Publication Data
Mochizuki, Ken.
Be water, my friend : the early years of Bruce Lee / by Ken Mochizuki ;
illustrated by Dom Lee. — 1st ed.
p. cm.
Summary: "A biography of Bruce Lee focusing on his early years in
Hong Kong, where he discovered martial arts and began developing the
physical and mental skills that led to his career as a legendary martial artist
and film star"—Provided by publisher.
ISBN-13: 978-1-58430-265-0   ISBN-10: 1-58430-265-8
1. Lee, Bruce, 1940–1973–Juvenile literature. 2. Actors—United States—
Biography—Juvenile literature. 3. Martial artists—United States—Biography—
Juvenile literature. I. Lee, Dom, 1959, ill. II. Title.
PN2287.L2897M63 2006
791.4302'8092–dc22
[B]   2005032205